By the Same Author

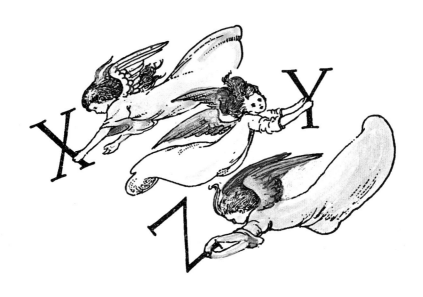

THE ANGELS'
ALPHABET

by

Hilda van Stockum

BETHLEHEM BOOKS · IGNATIUS PRESS
WARSAW, N.D.   SAN FRANCISCO

"For he hath given his angels charge over thee
To keep thee in all thy ways.
In their hands they shall bear thee up,
Lest thou dash thy foot against a stone."

ISBN 1-883937-24-8
Library of Congress catalog number: 96-85354

Cover art by Hilda van Stockum
Cover design by Davin Carlson

Bethlehem Books • Ignatius Press
R.R. 1 Box 137-A, Minto, ND 58261
1-800-757-6831

Printed in Canada

Dedicated
to
the dear overworked Guardian Angels of my children
to whom I owe
so
much

 is for Angels and Archangels

We are never alone in this wicked world.
There are always angels near,
And all of Heaven is watching us,
So we need never fear.

And when we do a kindly deed—
Sharing a toy with friends—
If we listen well we're sure to hear
The angels clapping their hands.

B is for Balaam's Ass

When Balaam went to prophesy
An angel barred the way
And Balaam's donkey balked the reins—
He could no more obey.

He could no more, he would no more
His master's blows in spite
Who, blind and angry, failed to guess
What caused the donkey's fright.

And so the prophet Balaam
For all he was so wise
Missed what was plainly visible
To a little donkey's eyes.

O little donkeys everywhere
Cheer up—if you are kind
You may behold what all the wise
Have vainly tried to find.

is for Cherubim

Tiny dewdrops
    Newly pearled
        Hold the image
            Of the world.

Cherubim
    Divinely stirred
        Hold the image
            Of God's word.

D is for Dominations

Other angels called Dominations
Are sent to destroy abominations.
With Virtues and Powers they rule the skies
And chase with their swords the Father of Lies.

For the battle of good against evil goes on
As long as a creature is left to be won
And gallantly angels will enter the fray
To salvage one soul for the Judgment Day.

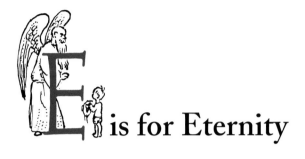 **is for Eternity**

My days are round as pennies
And roll as merrily
And they are all the wealth I need
To win Eternity.

But then I'll have to polish them
And keep them free from sin
For if my days are grubby
Saint Peter won't let me in.

Perhaps I'll even have enough
To help another boy
Who may have wasted all his days
Upon a silly toy.

I'll ask Saint Peter at the gate:
"Please, will you let him through?
I know he hasn't much to show,
But I've enough for two!"

# F is for Father

God has created stars and storms
And orchards and the sea,
He reigns above the golden clouds
In endless majesty.

And yet the littlest little child
Who toddles here below
May say "Our Father" to this king,
For Jesus taught us so.

 is for Gabriel

The angel Gabriel
Pierced the gloom
Of Our Lady's
Quiet room.

Where Our Lady
Bent her knee
Learning of the
Mystery.

Learning of the
Holy birth
Bringing Heaven
Down to earth.

And in sweet
Humility
Said: "Let it
Be done to me."

 **is for Heaven**

In Heaven I shall walk in God's gold light
With all the Blessed who are there
So many people I shall recognize
I'll smile and smile at old friends everywhere.

I'll meet the martyrs and the mighty saints
Whose lives I used to read with so much joy
And if I have been good, they'll shake my hand
And say: "We're pleased to meet you, little boy."

But, oh, if I have just missed being bad
Maybe they will not see me there at all
And pass me by, while talking of God's love.
Then I shall feel so very, very small.

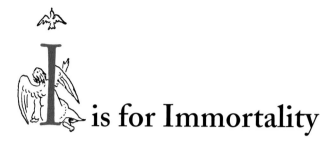

I is for Immortality

Our soul is like a little bird
Homesick for Heaven's skies,
And it will wing its way up there
When death has closed our eyes.

At least, if we have nourished it,
For though the soul can't die
Its wings may slowly waste away
And lose the strength to fly.

 **J** is for Jacob's Ladder

The sun had gone down
And stars were peeping
Over the head
Of Jacob sleeping.

Who saw a ladder
Raised to God
And up and down it
Angels trod.

While God Himself
On the ladder leant
Talking, to Jacob's
Wonderment.

And Jacob, listening,
Dimly guessed
How his offspring
Would be blessed.

Dimly guessed, for
From afar
He could see the
Christmas star.

 **is for Kingdom**

Christ drew a little child apart
And looked into its little heart.
He saw that it was free from guile
And so he gave a gentle smile
And told all grave and solemn men
They should be like that babe again:
As wondering and as meekly led
As trustful and as interested
As innocent of worldly sense
As free from every proud pretense
As near and friendly to the earth
As they were shortly after birth.
For in his kingdom there's no place
For people who take too much space.

 **is for Lamb of God**

O little innocent lamb of God
Who on his woolly coat
So sweetly bore the punishment
Of each wee, wicked goat,

What can the goats now do for you
Who did so much for them
Except bleat out their gratitude
To God's own, perfect Lamb?

 **M** is for Saint Michael

Whenever I fear
That the Devil is near,
Perhaps right under my bed,
I close my eyes tight
And with all my might
I think of Saint Michael instead.

Of the angels' choir
There's no one higher
He is the captain of all
And he'll be right there
With flaming hair
The minute I softly call.

The Devil he quakes
In his shoes he shakes
When he thinks of Saint Michael's sword.
For no gallant knight
Is so shining bright
As this champion of the Lord.

N is for Nevermore

It is not very long that we are here
And there's one little word I greatly fear:
That's "nevermore."
It will come when Saint Peter has opened the gate
When for something I still want to do it's too late—
Forevermore.

It might have been something to make God smile
Perhaps I'd kept putting it off for a while
Till I fell asleep.
Then, facing God, I'd search in vain
For that smile, though I'd look again and again.
Oh, how I'd weep. . . .

# O is for Obedience

The martyrs thought that dying was a treat.
We must look twice before we cross the street.

The saints but seldom saw a crust of bread.
When we refuse to eat we're sent to bed.

The pilgrims walked barefooted in the cold.
But when we take our shoes off people scold.

Though hemits often didn't wash for years
We children even have to clean our ears!

Is there no way for us at all
To be holy when we're small?

Yes, in God's eyes it's purest gold
Always to do as you are told

Not poutingly or in a rage
But like God's loving little page.

# P is for Principalities

The guardian angels are the humblest of all.
They look after people like me.
And if they should only forget for a day
In what a bad fix we should be.

Yet do we thank them for all their care
For watching the whole night through?
No, we only make it so hard for them
They often don't know what to do.

Then they go to the Principalities
Who command all the angels below
And if there is any way out at all
The Principalities will know.

But even the Principalities
Can't cure an evil will
And that's why with all those angels around
The world is wicked still.

 **is for Queen of the Angels**

She was only a little girl
Though full of grace
And, oh, without her shining face
Heaven would be a duller place.

She was only a little girl
But it is helpless we should be
Without her love for you and me,
Her pleading for us endlessly.

Because she was a little girl
There's no one else to understand
Or be so ready to defend
As she, the Queen, who is our friend.

 is for Raphael

God's own healer
Raphael,
Come and make my
Baby well.

You who brought
Tobias aid,
Banished from his eyes
The shade,

Look upon this
Bit of woe
Tossing wildly
To and fro . . .

Little laddie
Can't lie still
He feels far and far
Too ill.

And he is so
Dear to me,
Angel, won't you
Hear our plea?

Blessed angel
Raphael,
Come and make my
Baby well.

 S is for Seraphim

Who is loving God
When we're busy
Or when we're dancing
Ourselves dizzy?

Who is loving God
When we're sad
Or bored, or angry,
Or just plain bad?

Who is loving God
When we are deep
In our books or fast
Asleep?

Who is loving God?
The Seraphim.
Their charity
Will never dim.

Like candles they glow
Before God's face
Making up for our
Lack of grace.

 **is for Thrones**

The angels called Thrones are near the Most High
Whom with seraphs and cherubs they glorify
     And praise
While the lower choirs are on the wing
Doing any and everything
     He says.

We are surrounded by unseen friends
And helped by a hundred unearthly hands
     Every day
While messengers carry on golden wings
Our feebled words to the King of Kings
     When we pray.

 **U** is for: "unto the least of these."

What you do unto the least of these, Christ said,
Is done to me, is done to me instead.

O little things, O least things everywhere
For His sake I'll be tender, I'll take care.

All chicks and puppies will be safe with me
And any captive birds I shall set free.

And I'll be watching where I walk, in dread
Of stepping on a little beetle's head.

Not shall I dare to laugh in mockery
At anyone, for fear it should be He.

O little things, O least things everywhere
Let anyone who slights or injures you, beware.

Lest He who was so little here below
Should cry out later: "Oh! He hurt me so!"

 **V** is for Virtues

Virtues are the angels whom God puts in charge
Of every unusual event.
They manage His wonderful miracles
Which summon us all to repent.

If ever I am an angel one day
I should like to be one of these.
And rescue poor saints from a tyrant's claws,
Blowing pathways right through the seas.

I should like to bewilder a wicked king
And send toads hopping over his throne,
But I fear I'd be tempted just once in a while
To work miracles all on my own.

And, oh, what a terrible muschief there'd be
If one angel didn't obey,
Turning good into bad and day into night
And everything every which way.

 **is for the Word of God**

I love God's word, God's loving word
    When shorn
Of all its glory it reached earth
    Newborn.

When in a night with stars all hushed
    With awe
God's word was just a whisper
    In the straw.

 **is for Xmas**

X used to be the Greek letter for Christ
And in Xmas it's written so yet
Putting a cross in the happy word
Like a shade over Christ's bassinet.

X is also the symbol for what is unknown
And no one knew Him at all
Who was expected with royal pomp
And came as a babe in a stall.

I only wish I had lived that day
and had heard the angels' song.
I would have hurried across the hills
Bringing my toys along.

I would have hurried across the hills
Wherever the big star led,
To kneel down at the baby's feet
And give Him all I had.

 is for Yoke

Christ said His yoke was easy and His burden light.
      How can that be
When He wants us to be so very good
      Better than me?

When we must always choose the smallest piece
      And never fight
But smile when people call us horrid names
      And stay polite.

When we're to be forever giving thanks
      And mayn't complain
Even when our newest Sunday hat
      Is spoilt with rain.

How can His yoke be easy? Ah, if you
      Would only wear it,
You'd see how ready all the angels are
      To help you bear it.

 is for Zeal

Zeal is the magic spark which lights
My angel through the lonely nights
When stars are bright and shadows deep
And I am fast and fast asleep.

Blessed be God

In His angels

And in His saints.